Leader's Guide
for a study course on

What Happens When Women Pray

by Evelyn Christenson

Leader's Guide prepared by
EVELYN CHRISTENSON and
EMILY NICHOLSON

Instructions and 12 transparency masters (or visuals)
included in a removable center section.

Eleventh printing, 1984

VICTOR
BOOKS a division of SP Publications, Inc.
WHEATON, ILLINOIS 60187

Offices also in
Whitby, Ontario, Canada
Amersham-on-the-Hill, Bucks, England

ISBN: O-88207-943-3
© 1978 by SP Publications, Inc.

Suggested Teaching Methods

Brainstorming. Announce the question or topic to be "stormed." Members make as many informal suggestions as possible, not waiting to be called on. No criticism of suggestions is allowed. List suggestions on board; when all are in, have class evaluate and discuss the ideas. This method loosens up the group, involves nonparticipants, and produces new ideas.

Buzz Groups. Divide the class into groups, with from three to six persons, depending on size of class, in a group. Appoint a leader for each group or let groups select own leaders. Assign a topic to each group. Several—or all—groups can discuss same topic if necessary. Allow 5-8 minutes for discussion in the groups, then reconvene entire class and get reports from group leaders. Jot findings on board for discussion by entire class. Many persons are freer to express themselves in small groups, so this method provides maximum participation and interaction.

Discussion. Not to be confused with *Question and Answer.* In discussion, members react not only with the teacher but with one another. Usually discussion is started by the teacher asking a question to which there is more than a single acceptable answer. ("Where was the Sea of Galilee?" is hardly a discussion question!) A student will respond to a question, someone else may disagree with him, and a third person may have additional comments. The teacher is responsible for starting the discussion, keeping it "on track" by asking leading questions as necessary, and summarizing it after contributions cease. If a discussion gets out of hand and rambles, much of its value is lost.

Group (or Class) Bible Study. Each person should have his Bible open. Ask questions that will help the class learn what the passage you are studying says. Encourage sharing of insights as group discusses the interpretation of the passage and its application to current needs. Always summarize findings. This method makes students think; it shows them how to study the Bible on their own; and it increases participation and involvement.

Interview. Ask questions—or have someone in the class ask questions—of the person being interviewed. He will ordinarily be a "resource" person—one who has a fund of specialized knowledge on which you will draw. Or, an interview can be a variation on *Role Play* (see page 3).

Lecture. Needs no definition! If you lecture, aim to be *interesting*—well-prepared, enthusiastic, cordial, relevant, and with perhaps a touch of humor when it is in good taste.

Listening Groups. Same as *Buzz Groups,* except that each group is assigned a topic to listen for as someone reads a selection—Scripture or something else—or discusses a subject. When the class is reassembled as a whole, group leaders report and then the entire class evaluates the reports.

Neighbor Nudging. Like *Buzz Groups,* except that there are only two people, sitting next to each other, in each "group." In couples' classes the neighbors can be man-and-wife teams, or you may want to have the men on one set of teams and the women on another. (If a person is left out in the pairing off, assign him to one of the twosomes.) This method makes it easy for bashful persons to participate. However, since there are no group leaders, it may be hard to get some "neighbors" to speak up in the general session following the nudging.

Question and Answer. Teacher asks questions and students answer them. Makes for good interaction between teacher and students. Teacher should word questions carefully in advance—imprecise, confusing questions will be the death of this method, which provides involvement, guides group thinking, and keeps the class on the assigned topic, preventing "wandering."

Reading Groups. Same as *Buzz Groups or Listening Groups,* except that members of the group are assigned a passage of Scripture (or something else) to read and are given questions to be answered on the basis of the selection. The entire class then discusses the reports of the groups. In *Reading Groups* there are ordinarily no leaders, though in larger groups they may be helpful.

Skit. Have members read the parts of a brief script that highlights a point, provokes discussion, or presents information. Provides good variety.

Role Play. Two (or more) class members, without advance notice or written scripts, act out a situation or relationship. Give them directions as to the kind of people they are to represent and the situation in which they find themselves. They speak extemporaneously. Follow with analysis and evaluation by the class. This method helps people "feel" situations, gives them opportunity to try different solutions, and creates interest at the beginning of class. Helps apply Scripture to interpersonal relationships.

Study Groups. Like *Buzz Groups,* but instead of discussing a subject, the groups study a passage, examining it for what it says, what it means, or how it may best be applied. Each group has a leader.

Discussion is by far the best single method. If your group participates well in discussion, you will have little need for the other methods—which, after all, are designed primarily to stimulate discussion. If your class sits glumly silent instead of getting into a discussion, use other methods indicated to loosen them up.

Here are a few rules for leading discussion:
1. Maintain a relaxed, informal atmosphere.
2. Don't call on people by name to participate unless you are quite sure they are willing to do so.
3. Give a person lots of time to answer a question. If necessary, restate the question casually and informally.
4. Acknowledge any contribution, regardless of its merit.
5. Don't correct or otherwise embarrass a person who gives a wrong answer. Thank him; then ask the class, "What do the rest of you think?" or, "Has someone else another view?"
6. If some individual monopolizes the discussion, say, "On the next question, let's hear from someone who hasn't spoken yet." If necessary, ask the "monopolizer" privately, after class, to give other people more time to answer questions.
7. If someone goes off on a tangent, wait for him to draw a breath; then say, "Thanks for those interesting comments, Joe. Now let's get back to . . ." and mention the subject under consideration, or ask or restate a question that will bring the discussion back on target.
8. If someone asks a question, allow others in the group to give their answers before you give yours.

General Preparation

Survey the entire *Text* and this *Leader's Guide*. *This is basic*. Underline important passages in the text and make notes as ideas come to you, before you forget them. Become familiar with the entire course, including all units in the *Guide* that you will be using in your study. A general knowledge of what is coming up later will enable you to conduct each session more effectively and to keep discussion relevant to the subject at hand. If questions are asked that will be considered later in the course, postpone discussion until that time.

Add to your teaching notes any material and ideas you think important or of special help to your class. As teacher, your enthusiasm for the subject and your personal interest in those you teach, will in large measure determine the interest and response of your class.

We recommend strongly that you plan to use teaching aids, even if you merely jot down a word or two on a chalkboard from time to time to impress a point on the class. When you ask for a number of answers to a question, as in brainstorming, always jot down each answer in capsule form, to keep all ideas before the group. If no chalkboard is available, use a magic marker on large sheets of newsprint over a suitable easel. A printer can supply such paper for you at modest cost.

Once you have decided what visual or audio aids you will use, make sure *all* the necessary equipment is on hand *before* classtime. If you use electrical equipment such as projector or recorder, make sure you have an extension cord available if needed. For chalkboards, have chalk and eraser. That's obvious, of course, but small details are easily forgotten.

Encourage class members to bring Bibles or New Testaments to class and use them. It is good to have several modern-speech translations on hand for purposes of comparison.

Getting Started Right

Start on time. This is especially important for the first session for two reasons. First, it will set the pattern for the rest of the course. If you begin the first lesson late, members will have less reason for being on time at the others. Those who are punctual will be robbed of time, and those who are habitually late will come still later next time. Second, the first session should begin promptly because getting acquainted, explaining the procedure, and introducing the textbook will shorten your study time as it is.

Begin with prayer, asking the Holy Spirit to open hearts and minds, to give understanding, and to apply the truths that are studied. The Holy Spirit is the great Teacher. No teaching, however orthodox and carefully presented, can be truly Christian or spiritual without His control.

Involve everyone. The suggested plans for each session provide a maximum of participation for members of your class. This is important because—

1. People are usually more interested if they take part.
2. People remember more of what they discuss together than they

do of what they are told by a lecturer.
3. People like to help arrive at conclusions and applications. They are more likely to act on truth if they apply it to themselves than if it is applied to them by someone else.

To promote relaxed involvement, you may find it wise to—
1. Have the class sit in a circle or semicircle. Some who are not used to this idea may feel uncomfortable at first, but the arrangement makes class members feel more at home. It will also make discussion easier and more relaxed.
2. Remain seated while you teach (unless the class numbers over 25).
3. Be relaxed in your own attitude and manner. Remember that the class is not "yours," but the Lord's, so don't get tense!
4. Use some means to get the class better acquainted, unless all are well-known to each other. At the first meeting or two each member could wear a large-lettered name tag. Each one might also briefly tell something about himself, and perhaps tell what, specifically, he expects to get from this study.

Adapting the Course

This material is designed for quarterly use on a weekly basis, but it may be readily adapted to different uses. Those who wish to teach the course over a 12- or 13-week period may simply follow the lesson arrangement as it is given in this *Guide,* using or excluding review/examination sessions as desired.

For 10 sessions, the class may combine four of the shorter lessons into two. The same procedure should be followed for five sessions. However, if the material is to be covered in five sessions, each one should be two hours long with a 10-minute break near the middle. Divide the text chapters among the sessions as needed.

An Alternate Approach

The lesson plans outlined for each session in this *Guide* assume that class members are reading their texts before each class meets. The teacher should make every effort to spark interest in the text by giving members provocative assignments (as suggested under each session) and by such methods as reading aloud an especially fascinating passage (very brief) from the next week's text.

When for any reason, most of the class members will *not* have read the text in advance, (as when the class meets each evening in Vacation Bible School and members work during the day, or as in the first session, when texts may not have been available previously), a slightly different procedure must be followed.

At the beginning of the period, divide the class into small study groups of from four to six persons. Don't separate couples. It is not necessary for the same individuals to be grouped together each time the class meets— though if members prefer this, by all means allow them to meet together regularly.

As teacher of the class, lead one of the study groups yourself. Appoint a leader for each of the other groups. If people are reluctant to be leaders, explain that they need not teach and that they need no advance knowledge of the subject.

Allow the groups and their leaders as much as half an hour to study the textbook together. Then reassemble the class. Ask leaders to report findings or questions of unusual interest or that provoked disagreement. Ask the class the questions you want discussed, and allow questions from your students. Be sure to summarize, in closing, what has been studied. Finally, urge each member of the class to make some specific application of the lesson to his life. Use any of the material in this *Guide* that is appropriate and for which you have time.

Prayer Is the Answer / *Text, Chapter 1*

Determine Your Goals

To motivate group members for this study on prayer, and help them realize that merely knowing the philosophy of prayer is not enough; to experience the thrill of having their prayers answered, they must actually pray.

Preparation

Read the entire text, including the table of contents, then go back and reread chapter 1. Scan sessions 1—12 of the guide so you will know what Scriptures and aspects of prayer are reserved for future sessions. Acquaint yourself with all the MTMs, noting the one for this session. Then concentrate on the particular teaching on prayer that is presented in chapter 1 in the text.

Examine and Share

1. Welcome everyone and express your excitement about the course. Admit that you too are a learner in the school of prayer, and you are looking forward to many happy experiences in actually praying with the group and rejoicing together as you see God answer prayer. Begin the session with prayer.

2. Ask the group to mention reasons they have heard Christians give for praying or not praying. Include the following:

- I seldom pray anymore because God never seems to answer me.
- I pray because people expect me to, but I don't really look for God's answer.
- I pray because I find prayer exciting as I see God answer many of my prayers.
- I pray because God has told me to and I want to know Him better.
- I don't pray because I frankly can't see that it makes any difference whether I pray or not.
- I pray because it is a psychological release for my emotions.
- I pray because things happen when I pray that don't happen if I skip praying.
- I pray only about the big things because I don't feel I should trouble God about the mundane affairs of my life.

3. Ask group members to record in their notebooks (while you do the same) their honest feelings about prayer. Tell them that being honest with God and feeling their own need are two prerequisites of true prayer, which God always answers. Then ask the group to write down what they want God

to do for their prayer lives during this course of study.

4. Discuss the following question for about five minutes: *Why is prayer so often a last resort with Christians?* Final conclusions of the group should include: Christians don't really feel their need of God because they are convinced they can handle things by themselves (recount author's testimony on pages 9-10 in the text; it's easier to talk about prayer and to make our own plans than it is to pray first and then plan, trusting God to guide our planning sessions (briefly tell the incident described on pages 12-13 in the text).

5. Divide into three Bible study groups (see *Guide,* p. 2) for a Scripture search of circumstances changed through prayer: 2 Kings 20:1-11; Acts 12:1-17; James 5:16-18. Each group should study one of the Scripture passages, using the following questions typed on a 3″ x 5″ card. (a) What were the circumstances and the emotions produced? (b) Who prayed? (c) How did God change circumstances because of prayer? (d) Do you have one prayer answer to share with the group?

After 7 to 10 minutes, reconvene into a large group and ask a spokesman from each group to report the results of their Bible search.

Encourage airing of feelings, and ask questions such as, *But does God still intervene in affairs today? Does He really help us out of life's tangles?* (He does.) Ask your group to evaluate the statements: "I really prayed, but God didn't seem to hear or answer—certainly nothing spectacular happened," and, "When things change today, it might just be the result of natural causes, not because God has taken a hand in the circumstances."

Always aim for honesty of expression (the Psalms are our textbook in honest expressions of feelings), but never allow a discussion to end on a negative note. *God is always victorious; God always has the answer.* Our part is to find it in His Word and abide by His decisions.

Challenge each person by asking: *Is your prayer life all you want it to be? Is your prayer life all God wants it to be? Are there any missing dimensions in your prayer life?*

To establish a feeling of need, each person may look up these Scriptures about prayer: 1 John 5:14-15, *Am I praying in God's will?* James 4:1-3, *Am I asking amiss (with the wrong kind of aim)?* Hebrews 11:6, *Am I asking in faith?*

Individuals may record the Scriptures and questions in their notebooks, then write what they want God to do in their prayer lives this week.

Pray as Members of Christ's Body, the Church

Don't just talk about prayer but get the people involved in praying. Display MTM-1 as you discuss the thrill of being plugged into God's power through prayer.

Mention that you are going to divide into groups of approximately four people. Each group will observe the following rules which will apply throughout the entire study:

- No one needs to pray out loud if he doesn't want to.
- Each person prays out loud if he wishes to do so, taking turns praying

one sentence only. No one is to pray more than one short sentence.

Divide into the small groups. The leader of the small group may begin by leading the group in the kind of prayer they will pray. For example: "Dear God, teach me to plug into Your power. Amen."

The brief prayers of the eight chairpersons in the beginning of the chapter (*Text*, p. 10) are also good examples of the kind of praying the leader should encourage. Mature pray-ers need to learn to pray short prayers. Much long praying in a group originates in *pride* and should be avoided as it will kill the spirit of a group which is made up of both immature and mature Christians.

Assignment

Read chapter 2 in the text. Each person should record in his notebook time spent with God each day, prayer requests and answers, whatever God says to him, and his own feelings and attitudes.

Ask a group member to prepare a three-minute report on the reasons the author related for why it took her, and the women she was leading, so long to learn to pray effectively.

SESSION **2**

It Doesn't Take So Long / *Text, Chapter 2*

Determine Your Goals

To help group members recognize that unconfessed sin is a barrier between them and God, and to lead them to confess and forsake sin so they can be effective intercessors.

Preparation

Read this chapter and apply the truth to your own life. Settle any accounts with God and others so you can be an effective instrument in the hands of the Holy Spirit as you lead the group. Ditto a copy of MTM-2 for each group member (see "Other Uses of Transparency Masters" in center of *Guide*). Type out a copy of the main points in the *Pray in Secret* section in this session for each person. During the week, check with the person you asked to prepare a report on the reasons the author related for why it took her and the women she was leading so long to learn to pray effectively.

9

Type out references mentioned under *Preparation,* 6.

Examine and Share

1. Begin the session with prayer.

2. Ask the group to brainstorm (*Guide,* p. 2) the question: *Why doesn't God answer prayer?* List the reasons on the chalkboard.

3. Ask for the assigned report (see *Preparation*).

4. Point out the conditions of effective prayer, as related in this chapter (James 5:16b): (a) *Prayer*—true concern for the person or situation being prayed for—women praying for their children when witchcraft was being taught in the high school; (b) *Fervency*—shedding of tears over others— "April praying"; (c) *Righteous person*—confession of sin.

5. Conduct a Scripture search of two classes of sins: (a) John 16:7-9— Jesus said the Holy Spirit will convict the world of sin, namely, "Those who don't believe on Me." Church membership, creeds, rituals have nothing to do with believing on Jesus. Jesus is talking about those who need to believe in Him as Saviour and Lord. (b) Psalm 66:18; Isaiah 59:1-2; 1 Peter 3:12 —sins which Christians commit. Ask, *How do we know Christians sin?* (Our daily experiences show it; 1 John 1:8 proves it.) *How may Christians deceive themselves about the sin problem?* (By pretending they are sinless. Note, verse 8 does not say they deceive *others* about their sins.) *How may a sinning Christian receive forgiveness?* (1 John 1:9—by confessing his sin and believing he is forgiven.)

6. Give each person a copy of MTM-2. As various group members read their assigned Scriptures (have references typed out ahead of time), individuals may write on their copy of the MTM the sin mentioned.

Say: *Every yes answer is a sin in your life that needs to be confessed.* (Read James 4:17.)

Read 1 Thessalonians 5:18. Do you worry about anything? Have you failed to thank God for *all* things, the seemingly bad as well as the good? Or are you calling God a liar by not believing His Word? Do you neglect to give thanks at mealtimes?

Read Ephesians 3:20. Do you fail to attempt things for God because you are not talented or wise enough? Do feelings of inferiority keep you from trying to serve God? When you accomplish something for Christ, do you fail to give Him all the glory?

Read Acts 1:8. Have you failed to be a witness with your life for Christ? Have you felt it was enough to just live your Christianity and not witness with your mouth?

Read Romans 12:3. Are you proud of *your* accomplishments, *your* talents, *your* family? Do you fail to see others as better than yourself, more important than yourself, in the body of Christ? Do you insist on your own rights? Do you think as a Christian you are doing quite well? Do you rebel at God wanting to change you?

Read Ephesians 4:31. Do you complain, find fault, argue? Do you have a critical spirit? Do you carry a grudge against Christians of another group because they don't see eye-to-eye with you on all things? Do you speak unkindly about people when they are not present? Are you angry with yourself? Others? God?

Read 1 Corinthians 6:19. Are you careless with your body? Are you guilty of not caring for it as the temple of the Holy Spirit, in eating and exercise habits? Do you defile your body with unholy sex acts?

Read Ephesians 4:29. Do you ever use filthy language, tell slightly off-color jokes? Do you condone others doing so in your presence, in your home?

Read Ephesians 4:27. Do you fail to see you are a "landing strip" for Satan when you open your mind to him through TM, yoga, seances, psychic predictions, occult literature and movies? Do you get advice for daily living from horoscopes rather than from God? Do you let Satan use you to thwart the cause of Christ in your church through criticism, gossip, nonsupport?

Read Romans 12:11. Do you fail to pay your debts on time? Avoid paying them altogether? Do you charge more on credit cards than you can pay when due? Do you neglect to keep honest income tax records? Do you engage in any shady business deals either as an employer or employee or self-employed person?

Read 1 Corinthians 8:9. Do you feel you can do anything you want to because the Bible says you are free in Christ? Even though you were strong enough not to fall, do you fail to take responsibility for a weaker Christian who has fallen because of following your example?

Read Hebrews 10:25. Are you irregular or spasmodic in church attendance? Do you attend preaching services in body only, whispering, reading, or planning while God's Word is being preached? Are you skipping prayer meeting? Have you neglected family devotions?

Read Colossians 3:9. Do you ever lie? Exaggerate? Overcharge? Do you fail to see "little white lies" as sin? Do you tell things the way you want them rather than the way they really are?

Read 1 Peter 2:11. Are you guilty of a lustful eye toward the opposite sex? Do you feed your mind on sex-oriented TV programs, movies, books, magazines? Their covers? Do you indulge in any lustful activity God's Word condemns—fornication, adultery, perversion?

Read John 13:35. Are you guilty of being a part of divisions in your church? Would you rather add fuel to a misunderstanding than help correct it? Have you loved only the ones in your own church, feeling those of other denominations are not of the body of Christ? Are you secretly pleased over the misfortunes of another? Annoyed by his successes?

Read Colossians 3:13. Have you failed to forgive anybody anything he might have said or done against you? Have you turned people off? Are you holding grudges?

Read Ephesians 4:28. Do you steal from your employer by doing less work, staying on the job less time, than you are paid for? As an employer, do you underpay?

Read Ephesians 5:16. Do you waste time? The time of others? Do you spend time watching TV trash, reading cheap books, procrastinating?

Read Matthew 6:24. Is your goal in life to make as much money as possible? Accumulate things? Have you withheld God's share of your income from Him? Is money your god?

Read Matthew 23:28. Do you know in your heart you are a fake, just pretending to be a real Christian? Are you hiding behind church membership to cover a life still full of sin? Are you faking Christianity for social status, acceptance in your church, community? Do you smile piously during the Sunday sermon but live in your sin all week? Are you the person in your home that you are trying to impress people you are?

Read Philippians 4:8. Do you enjoy listening to gossip? Passing it on? Do you believe rumors or partial truths, especially about an enemy or your competitor? Do you neglect to spend time every day reading the Bible? Do you fail to think on the things of God—the good and true and pure things— always?

Pray as Members of Christ's Body, the Church

Divide into groups of four people. Allow a time of silence while people listen to God speaking to them about the sins just uncovered through the Scripture reading.

Caution the group: When confessing sins aloud, don't say anything you'll regret mentioning when you leave this place. Be sure to use the word "forgive" in your prayer. You're not just asking God to help you "not be angry again"; you're confessing a specific sin for which you need to accept God's forgiveness.

Leader begins: "I confess [specific sin] as *sin.*

Others may pray one sentence, confessing sin. Be specific, if not too personal—sins of pride, hate, and so forth.

Pray in Secret

Give each person a copy of the following points for his notebook:

Purpose of scriptural meditation: To face up to specific barriers between me and God, and to do something about them.

Scriptures: Use the ones on your copy of MTM-2.

Meeting with God: (1) Read Scripture over and over until the Holy Spirit convicts you of specific *un*confessed sins; (2) List your sins, shortcomings, and failures in thought, word, and deed as the Spirit points them out; (3) Stay in God's presence till He brings a spirit of repentance; (4) Confess your sins, putting the specific sins into words. This will make you aware that all sin is against God (Ps. 51:4).

Recognize what Christ has done for you and *enjoy* the new life He has given you: John 8:36; 10:9-11; Romans 8; Hebrews 2:5-18; 4:11-15.

Assignment

Read chapter ~~1~~ 3 in the text. ~~Note change in chapter sequence~~ *sed bk,*

Forgiven as We Forgive | *Text, Chapter ~~11~~ 3*

Determine Your Goals

To help group members realize that Christ said three times that God won't forgive our sins, even if we've confessed them, *until* we forgive others. To give opportunity for individuals to forgive others.

Preparation

Note: This session is based on chapter 11 in the text. Reread the chapter and be sure you can teach it with a clear conscience. Ask a volunteer to be prepared to relate how the author learned this lesson of forgiveness. Be prepared to lead your group in discovering the eight steps of forgiveness found in 2 Corinthians 2:5-11. Carefully study the Scripture and let it speak to your own heart. Be familiar with chalkboard 1 and MTM-3.

Examine and Share

1. Pray for understanding of the Scripture passage.

2. Display MTM-3 as you conduct a Bible study on Matthew 6. In the Lord's Prayer, debts (transgressions) mean sins. Jesus asked God to forgive us our sin "as"—to the extent that—we forgive others.

3. When Jesus gave us the model prayer, He didn't stop at the end of the Lord's Prayer (Matt. 6:13) but used a connecting word *for* and added another thought (6:14-15).

4. Mark 11:24 is our prayer faith-verse. Jesus used the conjunction *and*. "And when you stand praying, forgive."

5. Study the eight steps of forgiveness found in 2 Corinthians 2:5-11. Ask for the assigned report on how the author learned to forgive.

The Apostle Paul was writing to the Corinthian church, which was torn by many internal problems and was harboring terrible sins. Paul had suffered much because of this church, for he loved it with a Christ-given love. Can't you feel his anguish as you hear him say in the letter: "Out of much affliction and anguish of heart I wrote unto you with many tears; not that ye should be grieved, but that ye might know the love which I have more abundantly unto you"? (2:4)

It was because Paul loved them so much that he couldn't bear for them or himself to live in sin, out of fellowship with the Lord and with one another. So he gave them a lesson in forgiveness (which is discussed and illustrated in the *Text*, one from which we can learn also.

Emphasize the seriousness of any Christian's harboring unforgiveness in his heart. Point out that such an attitude is especially serious when it involves people who are engaged in intercessory prayer, for sin blocks their prayers to God and Satan can gain an advantage and break up the prayer group.

6. Display and discuss chalkboard 1.

Pray as Members of Christ's Body, the Church

Divide into groups of four.

Leader prays out loud: "Dear God, bring to each of our minds one person who has grieved us and whom we have not forgiven." (See *Text*, p. 130.) Wait in silence about 30 seconds. Then ask members of the group to (1) pray in silence that God will forgive them the sin of not forgiving; (2) forgive that person in silence—under no circumstances should any name be mentioned aloud; (3) ask God for much love for that person—wait in silence and feel the love come into each heart. (4) Leader prays out loud that God will tell each person how to confirm that love to the forgiven one. (5) Group members should pray out loud, promising they will do what God told them to. (6) Leader closes in prayer: "Thank you, God, that everyone who has prayed this prayer has fulfilled Christ's teaching on forgiveness. Now we can claim forgiveness for sins we've confessed in the last session. We thank You for forgiveness."

Pray in Secret

Using a concordance, study the word *forgiveness* in the Bible. Write down in your notebook the Scripture references and what the verses say about God's forgiveness, Christ's forgiveness, and our forgiveness.

Memorize Ephesians 4:32 and rejoice in its truths: (1) God has forgiven me all my sins; (2) the old chains of unforgiveness and unlove are broken; (3) I am free to love and forgive others; and (4) Praise the Lord! Now pray for the person you have just forgiven.

Assignment

Read chapter 3 of the text.

If we don't forgive one another, God doesn't forgive us.	When we forgive others, God forgives us and removes any sin barriers between us and Him.

Chalkboard 1
Draw to show the seriousness of any Christian's harboring unforgiveness in his heart.

select prayer partners

Praying in One Accord | *Text, Chapter 3 4*

Determine Your Goals

To help group members realize the power there is in the body of Christ praying in one accord, and to lead them in actually participating in this exciting experience.

Acts 1: 9, 12-14

Preparation

Reread the chapter, studying the Scriptures on which the prayer principle is based. Plan how you will use the suggested teaching methods and chalkboard 2 and MTM-4. Type study questions on John 17 for group leaders to use. During the week, contact a few people and ask them to share with the group how God has answered their prayers which they began praying during the first session. This sharing of answered prayer is important for mutual encouragement, and fosters more faith in God and His willingness to answer prayer.

Examine and Share

1. Begin the session with prayer. Ask the people you contacted to share their requests and answers. Ask if any others wish to relate an experience they have had recently when God answered their prayers.

2. Ask, *What are the principles of praying in one accord as discussed in the Text?* (Prayer is to be in Jesus' name—Matt. 18:20 and *Text,* pp. 30-31; prayer is simple conversation with God, our Father—Matt. 6:9 and *Text,* pp. 31-32; prayer is to be in one accord—that is, pray only about one subject at a time with one person praying aloud while the others in the group are praying silently on the same subject—Acts 1:9, 12-14 and *Text,* pp. 29-30, 36-37.) As the group finds the principles (they may look through the chapter if they wish), list them on the chalkboard. A volunteer should read the Scripture on which the principle is based after it has been mentioned. Comment on each principle "as the Spirit leads."

3. Divide into small groups for Bible study based on Jesus' prayer for the unity of all believers (John 17) for 7-10 minutes. Give each leader a copy of the following questions. (a) How many times does Jesus pray that believers will be one as He and the Father are one? (vv. 11, 21-23) (b) Did Jesus pray this only for His followers who were alive that day or is this for believers today? (v. 20) (c) When Jesus ascended to heaven, how did His inner circle *practice* unity? (Acts 1:8—they held a 10-day prayer meeting.) Display MTM-4. (d) Is your view of unity that men, women, teenagers pray separately in their own groups? How would you define "in one

accord"? (Men and women, possibly teenagers, prayed together desiring the same thing.) (e) The result of that first 10-day prayer meeting was Pentecost (Acts 2:1). Can you expect changes in your group or organization if you practice this unity in prayer? (f) Will studying about prayer and/or memorizing Scriptures about prayer produce this unity or must it be actually praying in one accord to bring about such unity?

Pray as Members of Christ's Body, the Church

Divide into small groups.

Each should take turns praying the model prayer on page 37 of the *Text*.

He should pray one or two sentences, mentioning a need in his life or in the life of someone he knows. While one person prays aloud, others pray silently with and for the person.

Pray in Secret

Ask the group to study Jesus' high priestly prayer (John 17) and to record what God says to them as they study. Encourage them to keep their notebooks as a record of their relationship with the Lord. They should read the chapter several times, perhaps once a day for a week, till they feel some of the love Jesus and His Father feel for them warming their hearts. They especially should note the relationships mentioned in this chapter: between Jesus and His Father; believers and Jesus and His Father; believers and the world; believers and one another. As they meditate on Jesus' desire for unity and love among all believers, they could experience the Holy Spirit's conviction in certain areas of their lives. Perhaps they have been unloving to another believer; or wanted exclusive rights to God and have rejected from their love and company other believers who don't agree with them on all points of doctrine (not salvation, of course). As each person brings his own needs to God, He will answer and teach him to pray in one accord with other believers.

Assignment

Read chapter 4 in the text.

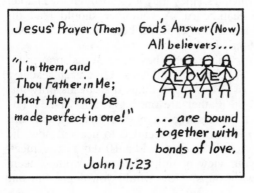

Jesus' Prayer (Then)   God's Answer (Now)
All believers...

"I in them, and
Thou Father in Me;
that they may be
made perfect in one!"

... are bound
together with
bonds of love,

John 17:23

Chalkboard 2
Use to illustrate we are one. We can pray in one accord.

The Method—Six S's / Text, Chapter *4* 5

Determine Your Goals

To help group members recognize the six S's of group prayer so that they can apply them to their prayer behavior in the group.

Preparation

Reread chapter 4 with more care than usual because you will be drawing heavily on it for background information. Don't hesitate to use illustrations from your own experiences or reading of other books on prayer. During the week, ask a group member to be prepared to relate the incident described in 2 Kings 19. Note chalkboard 3. Have a copy of MTM-5 for each person (see center of *Guide*) or make notebooks of three pages each following the pattern on MTM-5.

Examine and Share

1. Open the session with prayer.

2. Two volunteers may role play (see *Guide,* p. 3) a woman talking to her friend about why she doesn't want to come to a small prayer group. Both are Christians. The timid woman should mention her fears about praying in public, not knowing what to say, being embarrassed because mature pray-ers can pray on and on, and so forth.

3. Hand out copies of MTM-5 and display chalkboard 3.

a. *Subject by subject.* Members may name their own subjects and write them in their own notebooks.

Discuss planning "long prayers in advance." Ask, *How does this thwart praying in one accord? If you don't pray silently with the person praying aloud, are you better off praying alone, undisturbed?*

When we stay on one subject till finished, no one is deprived of the opportunity of praying about it. Review "Praying in One Accord"—praying with our hearts and minds on the same subject.

b. *Short prayers.* A volunteer may read Matthew 6:7-8. Discuss, *Why can someone who prays on and on kill the spirit of a prayer meeting? (Text,* pp. 41-43.) *What two things did Jesus say about praying long, repetitious prayers?* (That's pagan praying, God already knows everything.) *Are long prayers ever appropriate? If so, when?*

c. *Simple prayers.* Avoid high-sounding vocabulary. Tell incident of the Irishman (*Text,* pp. 43-44). If he can do it, can't you?

Look at Luke 23:39-43. Notice the urgency of the criminal's prayer. He had no time to pray a long prayer nor phrase his request "just right."

d. *Specific prayer requests.* As the group looks at 2 Kings 19, the volunteer you contacted during the week (see *Preparation*) may relate briefly the incident. Note Hezekiah's specific requests in verses 15-16, 19. The urgency of his need determined what Hezekiah asked the Lord for; perhaps our requests are vague because we feel no genuine need.

Discuss MTM-5. *What happens when we record and date requests?* (We remember we actually prayed about the request; this helps us be specific with God. We remember when we prayed for it.) *What happens when we record the answer and date?* (We praise God for answered prayer. We are encouraged to continue praying for other things. We find out how and when God really answers—not how we thought He was going to. This makes us realize we are important to God.)

e. *Silent periods.* Look at Psalm 27:14 and 46:10. *What do you do when there's a lull between audible prayers? Clear your throat? Shuffle your feet? Become embarrassed? Listen to God giving answers or directing to the next request?* Prayer is a two-way communication with God. *How do you feel if someone does all the talking? Frustrated? Angry? Turn them off? How do you think God feels when you do this to Him?*

f. *Small groups.* Have the group look at Matthew 18:19-20. *To whom did Jesus say this?* (Followers only.) *Why is it necessary for newcomers to be in small groups?* (People won't pray in large groups for the first time so small groups are imperative.) Discuss: *Where is Jesus' bodily presence now?* (Acts 7:55—Stephen saw Jesus standing at the right hand of God.) *In what way is Jesus in our midst?* (Matt. 18:20—He promised to be present.)

4. Start using the requests and answers in group members' notebooks. Give individual prayer requests so that they can be written with the date on the MTM sheet. Check the answers with the group next week and periodically after that.

Pray as Members of Christ's Body, the Church

Divide into small groups. Practice praying aloud and observing silent periods. Take turns praying one sentence out loud for each request announced—adding additional petitions to the original request. Pray fervently —length of prayer doesn't indicate fervency.

Chalkboard 3
Use to illustrate the six S's of prayer.

ubject by subject
hort prayers
imple prayers
pecific prayers
ilent prayers
mall groups

18

Instructions for Victor Multiuse Transparency Masters

As mentioned in the *Introduction to This Study* (*Guide*, p. 6), this removable center section provides Victor Multiuse Transparency Masters as important helps to your teaching this course. How transparencies can be made from them will be explained and instructions will be given for the specific use of each chalkboard or visual aid.

With educators' recognition of the teaching value of visual aids—even for adults—the Victor Multiuse Transparency Masters in this guide have been designed to give you maximum teaching help. They are numbered consecutively (MTM-1, etc.) and are coded to refer to both the guide and the text page numbers to which the illustrations relate. (The abbreviation **G**, followed by a number or numbers, refers to the page numbers in the leader's guide; the abbreviation **T**, followed by a number or numbers, refers to the page numbers in the textbook being studied.)

Some of the best visual aids available today are transparencies for overhead projection. Effective, creative teachers increasingly use transparencies to enliven class sessions and to transmit vital information to the mind through the eye-gate. Many churches already have overhead projectors, and each church should consider purchasing at least one, or one for each department. Ready-to-use transparencies are available and are becoming more so in the Christian education market, but they are expensive. However, you can make your own transparencies inexpensively through the use of transparency masters such as the ones in this guide.

Mechanics

Open up each of the staples carefully and pull out the sheets of illustrations and the one sheet of instructions. Close the staples again to keep your leader's guide together. Straighten out the illustration sheets by running a finger along the crease and file flat in a regular file folder (usually 9″ x 11¾″). Leave these instructions folded for easier reference (they are labeled as pages a, b, c, and d) and file with the transparency masters.

Making Transparencies from Masters

You can make transparencies in at least four ways:

1. *Thermal copier* (an infrared heat transfer process such as 3M's Thermofax). It is probably the fastest, most convenient, and best-known method. Simply pass the master with the appropriate film on top of the master through the copying machine (at the correct setting).

2. *Electrostatic process* (such as Xerox). Because of paper feeding requirements in these machines, care must be taken to have the correct film for the proper machine. Check before using. Also, the glass must be absolutely clean or all the dirt and dust particles will be picked up. The color on the MTM will come out gray.

3. *Photo-reflex process* (sometimes called the diffusion-transfer process). A wet process involving the exposure of a sheet of negative paper, placing it in contact with a sheet of positive paper or transparency film, and sending it through a processing machine (such as produced by Kodak, Agfa-Gevaert, and GAF Corporation).

4. *Trace your own on a transparency film.* (See below.)

Don't give up if your church does not have a copying machine. You likely live within a short distance of a machine. Try your public library, a school, or a secretarial service office (Copying or Duplicating Service in your Yellow Pages). Or maybe there's a machine at your office, or at a friend's. Usually arrangements can be made, either paying for the film or bringing your own.

You must be careful to have the right film for the right machine. To do so, first determine the type of copier that is available to you or to your friends. Then purchase the correct film from a local supplier (if not available with the machine), either an office supply house or a school supply company. If neither of these is available to you, order *A Teacher's Guide to Overhead Projection* (1969, Technifax Education Division, Holyoke, Mass. 01040), which is an excellent manual describing the production and operation of transparencies and includes the company's descriptions and prices, or *The Overhead System: Production, Implementation, and Utilization* (1972, University of Texas Visual Instruction Bureau, Drawer W, University Station, Austin, Texas 78712), which includes a valuable appendix of addresses for sources of equipment and materials. *Use Your Overhead,* by Lee Green (Victor Books, 1979) is a most helpful manual on use and production of overhead materials.

An alternate use for the transparency masters in this guide is for you to trace your own transparencies from the masters. With minimum artistic ability required, you can place a sheet of film over the master (the sheet should be at least 10" x 7") and trace the major part of the illustration. Exactness is not necessary and stick figures (as in the chalkboards) can be traced over the printed figures; lettering can be done separately. (For best results use .005 acetate or .003 polyester either in 8½" x 11" sheets or in a roll that can be cut to appropriate size.)

To write on the transparencies, use a grease pencil, preferably white, or a felt-tip marking pen (see *Materials,* page c). Grease pencil is harder to erase and does not look as neat as the felt-tip pen. Take care, however, in purchasing felt-tip marking pens, for there are a number of different kinds on the market. For transparencies you must have either erasable or nonpermanent if you wish to reuse the film (these wash off with water or a damp cloth quite easily), or permanent if you want to reuse the same visual aid. You may want to make the basic image with the permanent pen and add other material as needed with the washable one.

A further advantage of tracing your own transparencies is that you can make overlays. You expose only one part of the illustration; then, as the discussion progresses you expose the rest of it in parts or sections.

Other Uses of Transparency Masters

1. *Ditto Masters.* Another use to which the transparency masters may

be put is making Ditto masters from which you can run off material for each member of your class. The basic process is the same as that used for overhead transparencies. The transparency master has a thermal spirit master placed over it and is then run through a thermal copier (such as a Thermofax machine). From the master as many copies as needed are then made on any Ditto or spirit machine. If a Thermofax machine is not available, then the transparency master may be traced or copied onto a Ditto master or mimeograph, run off on the respective machines, and copies distributed to the class.

2. *Visuals.* For small classes or home Bible classes, the transparency masters may be used just as they are as visual aids to the lesson. It would be helpful to tape them or glue them to a piece of cardboard (making copies of the illustration on the back) and then prop up the visual against some books or with a homemade prop behind it. You are then free to refer to it during the lecture or discussion as it stands on the table near you.

3. *Chalkboards.* You may also use the transparency masters just as you do the other chalkboards in the guide. Simply copy the illustration onto a chalkboard or flip chart and use it as needed in your presentation (see *General Preparation,* third and fourth paragraphs, *Guide,* p. 4).

The Use of Color

In all of the methods discussed above (except that of Visuals) the colors on the transparency masters are to serve as guides to the teacher in coloring his transparencies, dittos, or chalkboards. The colors will not reproduce in the various processes (except in the Xerox, where the color turns out to be a gray shading), but will serve as guides for emphasis and distinction as the teacher colors in his transparencies.

Materials

The following is a partial list of materials necessary for the maximum use of transparencies, either through a mechanical copying process or homemade.

1. *Transparency Film.* 3M Corporation makes clear transparency film for the infrared process, 100 sheets to a box. LABELON Projection Transparencies—Infrared, 100 sheets to a box (TR-85). Also available in kits, which include clear and colored acetates, pens, frames, grease pencils, and instructions.

2. *Ditto Masters.* 3M Corporation: Klean Write KEM-FAX Spirit Masters (No. 321-D); and Heyer's Thermal Spirit Masters (No. 450 Purple).

3. *Pens.* These are available in many colors, both permanent and washable (but make sure that the kind you get will write on acetate).

Permanent—Sanford's (Bellwood, Ill. 60104) Vis-à-Vis Sharpie Pens; Eberhard Faber's Projectachrome Overhead Projector Markers (permanent); and 3M Visual Products Transparency Marking Pens (permanent).

Washable—Sanford's Vis-à-Vis Visual Aid Pens; Eberhard Faber and 3M clearly marked "nonpermanent."

4. *Grease Pencils.* Widely available in any office supply store.

Victor Multiuse Transparency Masters for This Guide

The following are some brief suggestions for using the multiuse transparency masters in the leader's guide for *What Happens When Women Pray.* There is one transparency for each session.

MTM-1   (*Guide*, p. 8)—As you lead the group in praying, display to visualize the thrill of being plugged into God's power through prayer.

MTM-2   (*Guide*, p. 10)—Ditto a copy for each group member as a record of the kinds of sins Christians commit.

MTM-3   (*Guide*, p. 13)—Display as you conduct a Bible study on Matthew 6.

MTM-4   (*Guide*, p. 15)—Display to illustrate how Jesus' followers practiced unity after He returned to heaven.

MTM-5   (*Guide*, p. 17)—Ditto a copy for person, to be made into a prayer-request-and-answer notebook.

MTM-6   (*Guide*, p. 20)—Visualize paradox of having our desires granted as we pray in God's will—1 John 5:14-15.

MTM-7   (*Guide*, p. 24)—Display to show how we can confidently commit ourselves and everything in our lives to God.

MTM-8   (*Guide*, p. 26)—Illustration of "closet" praying—Matthew 6:6.

MTM-9   (*Guide*, p. 27)—Illustrates wrong concept of leaving God's presence when we leave our quiettime place—God shares our lives all day.

MTM-10   (*Guide*, p. 29)—Alerts us to the dangers of meditation apart from genuine Christian praying.

MTM-11   (*Guide*, p. 32)—Shows the horizontal dimension of prayer —how God hears our intercessory prayer and showers blessings on the recipient.

MTM-12   (*Guide*, p. 35)—Gives prayer chain rules—make a copy for each person.

Pray in Secret

Each person should record the six S's from the chalkboard in his notebook. Check out what he needs to be aware of in group prayer.

- Does he jump from subject to subject so that people are becoming confused as they try to pray with him?
- Is he using too much time?
- Are his prayers long and wordy, displaying his ability to express himself well in public and his familiarity with God?
- Are his prayers complicated because he doesn't think through what he wants to ask God?
- Does he feel compelled to tell God all about the request, not trusting that God knows all the details?
- Are his prayers vague because he doesn't feel the urgency of requests?
- When there is a silent period, does he jump in before the Holy Spirit's leading so that there will be no "waste of time"?
- Is he aware of Jesus' presence when he is praying in small groups so that he can pray with confidence?

This week each group member should practice waiting on God. This implies not only trusting in God and knowing He is working on one's behalf, but also being quiet and still in His presence and listening to Him for answers.

Assignment

Read chapter 6 of the text. (Optional: Using a concordance, look up the references to waiting on God in the Psalms. Look under the words *wait, waited, waiting.*)

SESSION **6**

How to Pray in God's Will / *Text, Chapter 5*

Determine Your Goals

To help group members get rid of wrong ideas they may have about God's will, and to introduce them to the joy, peace, and open doors they will experience as they bring themselves into conformity with God's will by praying sincerely, "Your will, Lord, not mine, be done."

Preparation

As you reread this chapter, examine your heart to be sure you are honestly praying and desiring that only the Lord's will be done in your life. Type the

19

following comments, one each on a 3″ x 5″ card, and give them to five people as they enter the room. (1) "If I pray that God's will be done in my life, I'm afraid He'll make me do something I don't want to do." (2) "My mother is very sick. If I pray that God's will be done, I'm afraid she'll die." (3) "My husband wants to move to another town where his business prospects are better, but I don't want to leave my friends and job. If I pray God's will be done, I know He'll make me back up my husband and move, and I'll be so unhappy." (4) "We're having trouble with our teenage son. If I pray for God's will to be done, I'm afraid He'll answer in a way that is different from my plans, and I won't be able to live with the result." (5) "I have always been afraid to pray that God's will be done because even as a child I was taught that God's will could never be the same as mine—it will always be the exact opposite of what I want to do."

Note chalkboards 4 and 5 and MTM-6. Ask a good reader to record on a cassette tape the testimony on pages 55 and 56 of the text (or record a true incident known to you when a person learned to pray for God's will, and the resulting blessing). If a cassette player is unavailable, simply have the testimony read at the appropriate time. Type out the questions for the Bible study groups (#4 under *Examine and Share*).

Examine and Share

1. State, "Many Christians think that to pray for God's will to be done means some of the following results." (Ask for the five above comments to be read.)

2. Show and discuss the "Wrong concept of God," chalkboard 4, which makes people afraid to pray for God's will to be done. Mention that we need to understand that God is a loving Father who *always wills* what is best for His children. Only He knows what is best for us because He is God and knows all things.

3. Show and discuss the "Right Concept of God," chalkboard 5, emphasizing the question: *How do you feel?*

4. Divide into small Bible study groups. Give a copy of these Scriptures and questions to each group. Put MTM-6 on the overhead projector.

   a. *1 John 5:14-15. What paradox do you see in these verses?* Discuss

Chalkboard 4
Draw to show a wrong concept of God.

20

MTM-6. (I am to pray my desires according to God's will if I want my prayers answered.) *If my will isn't the same as God's, who changes?* (See prayer Jesus taught—Matthew 6:9-10.) *What is the definition of "effectual" in James 5:16?* (See *Text,* p. 55. Contrast this with rewording your prayer requests. That is why we pray requests, not answers.) *What is the secret of resolving this paradox?* (We conform our desires to God's will.)

b. *Luke 22:40-46. What did the Lord Jesus ask His Father?* ("If Thou be willing, remove this cup [of suffering] from Me.") *Why do you think the Holy Spirit had this soul struggle of the Lord Jesus recorded for us?* (Possibly so that we can realize how He suffered in His humanity; He knows the painful struggles we sometimes have as we give over our wills to God the Father. The initial struggle is painful, but the end result is always joy and peace.) *What words indicate that Jesus brought His desires into conformity with the Father's will?* (Verse 42 "Nevertheless not My will but Thine be done." Note that it was in this complete surrender of Christ's will to the Father's that His obedience reached its highest perfection. Had He not learned obedience here, He could not have become our Saviour—Heb. 5:7-9).

c. *Luke 1:26-38. What might have been running through Mary's mind when the angel announced that she would have a child by the Holy Spirit?* (She wasn't married; Joseph, and the rest of the world, would think her immoral; such immorality in those days often meant being stoned to death; what would her family say? how would the neighbors react? and so forth.) *How did Mary show her complete acceptance of God's will for her?* (See v. 38.) *What was the result of Mary's submission to God's will?* (She was the human instrument through whom the Saviour came to earth.)

Reassemble into a large group; briefly bring out the main points of each Scripture passage, emphasizing again the paradox revealed in MTM-6. Suggest that each person inventory his own circumstances. *Is he as available as Mary?* Ask, *Can closed doors ever be God's will? Can closed doors ever be as important as open doors?* (See *Text,* p. 59.)

Pray as Members of Christ's Body, the Church

Divide into small prayer groups. Remind people to use the "six S" prin-

Chalkboard 5
Draw to show the right concept of God.

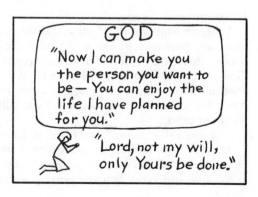

GOD

"Now I can make you the person you want to be — You can enjoy the life I have planned for you."

"Lord, not my will, only Yours be done."

ciples as they concentrate on today's prayer principle: praying for God's will to be done in them and in their sphere of influence.

Pray in Secret
Each person should record in his notebook Scripture references studied today. He should use them to evaluate his life in every area and relationship to see if he can pray for God's will to be done in each circumstance and relationship. Meditating on Luke 22:40-46 will give the strength to pray for God's will to be done.

Assignment
Read chapter 6 of the text.

God Never Makes a Mistake / Text, Chapter 6

Determine Your Goals
To help group members realize that God is a loving, omniscient Father who can use suffering to make them more Christlike and to whom they can pray with perfect confidence, knowing that God's answer will be for their good and the good of those for whom they are praying.

Preparation
Reread the chapter, asking God to make clear to you the reason for your own suffering (if you are or have). Study MTM-7. Decide how you will guide the discussion under #2 of *Examine and Share* and the conclusions the group should reach.

Examine and Share
1. Begin with prayer. Mention that the prayer principles they have studied, like many principles of knowing God in Scripture, are simple. The secret in making them work is found in actually practicing them; the secret of knowing God is in actually obeying Him as He reveals His will day by day. As we consider the truths in this lesson, we may find that we need to pray, "Lord, make me willing to be willing for Your will." God will then undertake for us in our need.
2. Lead a discussion (see *Guide*, p. 2) using these questions:
In what ways is God an omniscient Father to us? What effect does this characteristic of God have on the way He answers our prayers? (Text, p. 66) What is the difference between praying answers and praying requests? (Text,

pp. 67-68) *Why should we be thankful that God has given us a free will rather than just making us pawns in His hands?* (*Text,* p. 68) *How can we know whether we are asking "amiss" or are praying in the will of God?* (*Text,* pp. 68-70. Stay in God's Word—many answers will be found there. Are we abiding in Christ? Desiring to do His will? Wanting to be conformed to His image? Does the request glorify God? When God's Word doesn't give a specific answer, ask Him what His will is. The Holy Spirit, as Intercessor, then takes our request and prays according to the will of God— Rom. 8:26-27.) *Why should we be thankful when God says "No" to a request we wanted very much to have granted?* (*Text,* pp. 70-71)

3. Conduct a Bible study on suffering.

Hebrews 12:6-13—(a) *Define "chastening."* (Chastening is not punishment but discipline and teaching.) (b) *Who does the chastening?* (God.) (c) *How does this differ from God allowing suffering?* (God is doing something in our lives—the verb is active.) (d) *What two things can we be sure of when God disciplines us?* (God loves us; we are His children, v. 6.) (e) *What is the difference between the way earthly fathers discipline their children and the way God disciplines His?* (Earthly fathers discipline from their limited earthly perspective and out of the frailties of being human. See vv. 9-10. God disciplines out of His omniscience and love; always for our good.) (f) *What is the "afterward" for those who endure chastening with the right attitude toward their heavenly Father?* (The "peaceable fruit of righteousness," verse 11, that is, Christ's characteristics—Galatians 5:22-23, for example—are developed in them.) (g) *How should we help those who are enduring God's discipline at the moment?* (We can encourage them to endure and pray for them.)

Psalm 4:1—*Why does God send and/or allow suffering?* (To "enlarge us" and prepare us for the task ahead. Remember the open doors from last session?)

Psalm 119:71—*Why, according to this verse, is it good for us to be afflicted?* (Affliction sends us scurrying to His Word for answers.)

1 Peter 4:12-19—(a) *Is suffering ever the will of God for a Christian?* (*Text,* pp. 71-78) (b) *What kinds of suffering are mentioned in these verses?* (Suffering for Christ's sake—vv. 13-14, 16; suffering because of sin's consequences in our lives—v. 15; suffering as the result of judging ourselves as Christians—vv. 17-18.) (c) *How should Christians who are suffering for Christ's sake feel?* (Happy—vv. 13-14.) *Why?* (When His glory is revealed they will be glad with *exceeding joy*—v. 13b; God's Spirit is resting on them so they can bring glory to God through their suffering.) (d) *What should those who are suffering "according to the will of God" do?* (Commit themselves to God knowing He can handle things for them —v. 19.)

Romans 8:28—*For whose good is God working out all things in our lives —God's or ours? Have you come to the place where you really believe God never makes a mistake?* (God knows all the "what ifs"; He can handle things.) *Do you need to change your view of God as an omniscient Father?* (*Text,* p. 66)

James 1:2-4—(a) *Why are these verses not a misprint in the Bible?* (*Text,* p. 80) (b) *How should Christians feel when they have many temptations and testings?* (Joyful—v. 2) (c) *What does God want to do for us when we are experiencing trials and testings?* (God wants to make us into mature Christians who are growing up in Christ—vv. 3-4.)

Ephesians 5:20—(a) *Why should we give "thanks always, for all things unto God" no matter how difficult we may find it to be at times?* (*Text,* p. 80) (b) *How is "If it be Thy will" not just a phrase we tack on to the end of our prayers, if we want to be effectual intercessors?* (It expresses our heart's desire.) Display MTM-7.

Pray as Members of Christ's Body, the Church

Divide into small prayer groups. The leader should read the first paragraph, *Text,* page 81, and give members time to think. Instruct each person to pray aloud in his own words and in one sentence, paragraph two (identify aloud, if not too personal). Leader should lead the rest of the group in praying paragraph three aloud, then each should take turns praying it. Leader may read paragraph four and let members take turns praying it aloud.

Leader should close in prayer: Thank God that each one who has prayed the prayer has committed himself to God's will in every facet of his life and influence. He doesn't *desire* anything that isn't in conformity with God's will; thus 1 John 5:14-15 is true in his praying. The paradox is resolved because at this point he doesn't desire what isn't God's will and God will grant his desires.

Pray in Secret

Each person may record in his notebook the Scripture passages on suffering and the truth God is impressing on his heart for his own need. God can make James 1:2-4 and Ephesians 5:20 a reality.

Assignment

Read chapter 7 of the text.

SESSION **8**

The Space Dimension of Prayer—Where We Pray / *Text, Chapter 7*

Determine Your Goals

To teach that we can pray anywhere and in any posture, and to help draw up some guidelines for enjoying time alone with God each day.

'reparation

Reread the chapter. List some Scriptures that mean much to you because ;od revealed Himself to you through them in a special way, and be prepared) share a few such experiences with the group. Study Psalm 25, asking the ,ord to give you insights you can teach others. Check out MTM-8 and halkboard 6.

xamine and Share

1. Open the session with prayer. Ask group members to share requests nd dated answers from their intercessory prayer lists (MTM-5, Session 5).

2. Ask, *Does it matter to God where we are when we pray or what posi-on we assume?*

List the following Scriptures on the chalkboard for the group to look up nd tell the different places and postures of prayer mentioned. Jot their nswers on the board. *Luke 22:41*—Jesus knelt down. *John 11:41*—Jesus fted up His eyes. *Matthew 26:39*—Jesus fell on His face. *Mark 11:25*— tand praying. *Numbers 16:22*—Moses and Aaron prostrated themselves. *Chronicles 7:1-3*—Israelites bowed with their faces to the ground. *Psalm 34:2*—Lift up hands and bless the Lord. *1 Timothy 2:8*—Paul suggested 2ople pray *everywhere,* lifting up their hands. *Psalm 4:4*—King David rayed on his bed. *Daniel 6:10*—Daniel knelt down. *1 Kings 19:4*—Elijah it down under a juniper tree.

Prayer should be spontaneous, an overflow of our hearts; posture should 2 dictated by the need. Closing eyes in prayer is not a scriptural position, st a customary one.

Put chalkboard 6 on display. *Are you judgmental of people whose posture prayer differs from your customary one? Is your prayer posture really a riptural one? Would you be willing to try another scriptural posture?*

Share: *In what unusual postures and places have you prayed? Do you ink your need and kind of praying dictated the posture you assumed? Were you feeling guilty, submissive, filled with praise, adoring, etc.?*)

3. Conduct a Bible study on David's prayer which he prayed when he as in his secret place—Psalm 25. *What did David tell the Lord which re-aled his soulfelt trust in Him?* (vv. 1-2) *What did David ask for, which*

alkboard 6
e to display different praying sitions.

When you pray, enter your closet and shut the door (Matt. 6:6).

revealed his desire to be completely God's? (vv. 4-5a) *How do you know*
David was in the habit of talking to God and sharing his life with Him? (5b
How did David describe God? (vv. 6-8) *What is the characteristic of th*
person whom the Lord will teach? (v. 9) *What did David do, so that h*
could enjoy God's fellowship? (vv. 10-11) *What is the reward of fearin*
[trusting] the Lord? (vv. 12-13) *To whom does God reveal His secrets*
(v. 14)
  4. Display MTM-8. Discuss: *How does your closet praying affect you*
public praying? Describe a "closet"—yours or someone's you know abou
Do you have a special, holy spot where you meet God in a special way?

Pray as Members of Christ's Body, the Church
  Divide into small groups. Practice any scriptural position of prayer. N
one will judge anyone else for the position he assumes.
  Group leader should lead members to pray one prayer—either prayer o
page 88 of the *Text* or anything else God directs them to pray about.

Pray in Secret
  Encourage each member to use his secret place this week. Meditate o
Psalm 25 and its principles on meeting with God alone.

Assignment
  Read chapter 8 in the text.

The Time Dimension of Prayer—When We Pray | *Text, Chapter 8*

Determine Your Goals
  To help each person see the possibility of always being tuned in to Gc
and, as a result, learning to "pray without ceasing."

Preparation
  Reread the chapter. Ask a group member to be prepared to give a bri
talk on: "How I learned to begin the day with God." Think about MTM-9

Examine and Share
  1. Open the session with prayer. Volunteers may share their requests ar
dated answers from their intercessory notebooks (Session 5).
  2. Put this quotation on the chalkboard: "All of life should be a prayer
Invite discussion as to its meaning, and whether it is true or false. Sum

ae discussion by mentioning it is a takeoff on 1 Thessalonians 5:17: "Pray without ceasing." A Christian who is constantly tuned in to God is in a constant attitude of prayer. Such a Christian can talk to God at any time and is always in a receptive mood for God to talk to him or her. This doesn't mean Christian walks around with a pious expression or is afraid to laugh. It does mean that whatever such a person is doing or wherever he is, he is in contact with his Lord through the indwelling Holy Spirit.

Open communication with God brings one joy and peace which can only be understood by those who experience this relationship. It also frees one to really love and minister to others because God is in control of one's thought life. It makes God available for intercessory prayer at all times and keeps such a one available for God's nudge when He needs an intercessor on Planet Earth.

3. Ask for the talk on "How I learned to begin the day with God." Sum up what is said by the scriptural injunction to begin the day with God, whether one is a "lark" or an "owl" (*Text,* pp. 90-93; see Psalm 5:1-3). Discuss an owl vs. a lark—*which are you?* It doesn't matter whether you're an owl or a lark; what matters is that you spend time in your closet praying and giving your prime time to God.

4. Display MTM-9.

5. Mention the author's experience in getting her children off to school with happy remembrances of beginning the day asking for God's protection and direction (*Text,* pp. 93-94). Ask, *How does your child(ren) begin the day?*

6. Discuss: *Why should we pray, "Lord, give me the right attitude toward this person" when we come up against someone who rubs us the wrong way?* (See "The Day Progresses," *Text,* pp. 94-99.) Mention the SOS prayer which includes "look up" away from me toward God. Admit a wrong attitude and determine to want only God's will.

7. Relate how one woman who started the day with a rich time of worship with the Lord often found that during the day her spiritual "mood" bogged down with pressures, unexpected interruptions, and people who could be so difficult. She wondered why the peace she enjoyed during her time alone with God seemed to evaporate in the jarring realities of her life until she found the last part of verse 5, Psalm 25. Suddenly "on Thee do I wait all the day," caused her to realize that the morning sense of God's guidance was meant to be with her all the day as she waited on God (in her heart).

Pray as Members of Christ's Body, the Church

Divide into small prayer groups.

Talk about when to pray: Psalm 63:3—in the night watches; Psalm 5:1-3—in the morning; Ephesians 6:18—always, with perseverance and supplication for all saints.

Remind the group to apply the principles of the six S's as they pray.

Pray in Secret

Suggest that each person write out Psalm 25 in his notebook. Meet with

the Lord at the beginning of every day and make out an agenda in His pres
ence. Keep a record of how he progresses in learning to wait on the Lord al
day. Of course he will often need to change his agenda in part as the da
progresses, but the important thing is to ask God's guidance on each aspec
of his life and circumstances. Remind each one to keep tuned in constantl
to God so that he can "pray without ceasing" day or night.

Assignment
Read chapter 9 of the text.

The Vertical Dimension of Prayer—to Whom We Pray

Text, Chapter 9

Determine Your Goals
To make sure it is God in heaven to whom we draw nigh, to help u
realize the need for drawing close to God in silence till we sense His presenc
before we pray, and to guide the group in actually experiencing this closenes
to God in their prayer groups.

Preparation
Reread chapter 9. Prepare chalkboard 7 and think about MTM-10. Loo
up modern word equivalents of practices in Deuteronomy 18:10-11. Gath
newspaper ads, posters, and so forth of occult organizations (yoga, TM
witchcraft schools and meetings) in your community. Bring a horoscop
column from a local newspaper. If you know any Christian who has ex
perienced dealing with the dangers of the occult or anyone who has bee
helped out of occult involvement, ask him to speak briefly. Make a copy o
the Bible study questions for each small group.

Examine and Share
1. Begin with prayer. Talk about drawing close to God (James 4:8) an
put the following outline on the chalkboard:
   a. Come to God and wait silently before Him.
   b. Confess any sin that is separating me from God.
   c. Envision God in heaven—who He is; His love; power; concern for m
   d. Say, "Our God is in the heavens" (Ps. 115:3).
2. But we need also to be aware of "the god of this age" (2 Cor. 4:4
Ask the guest speaker to share the dangers of the occult, witchcraft, tra

28

endental meditation, and so forth, with the group. If you know of no one
ho can give such a talk, prepare a lecture (see *Guide*, p. 2) using the ma-
rial in the text, pages 105-109. Show ads, clippings and posters you col-
cted. Display MTM-10. It is most important that adults be aware of the
angers confronting junior high and high school young people today, not
mention the pitfalls into which gullible adults can fall as they seek "more
iritual experiences" without seeking more of the true God.

3. Display and discuss chalkboard 7.

4. Divide into small Bible study groups. Distribute the following to each
oup:

a. Make sure it is God to whom you have drawn nigh.

(1) Matthew 6:9. (a) *Why do you think Jesus taught His followers
to address their Father* in heaven *when praying?* (b) *Did Jesus understand
nd deal with a spiritual world we sometimes neglect to recognize?* (Discuss
Mark 1:21-27, 32-34, 35; 3:11-15, 22-30; 5:1-20; 6:1, 13.) (c) *Have
ou failed to see Satan and his demons as personalities capable of communi-
ating with us?*

(2) Deuteronomy 18:9-14. (a) Read the list of occult practices of
Moses' day in verses 10 and 11 from several good Bible translations. Make
re you understand the modern day equivalents. (b) Share experiences you
some family member or acquaintance may have had. (Limit discussion
you have time for the rest of the study.) (c) *Are these things or the people
ho practice them an abomination to God?* (d) Discuss how these practices
ould keep a Christian from drawing nigh to God (Deut. 18:20; 20:18).

(3) 2 Corinthians 4:4. (a) *In what ways can we communicate with
e god of this world today?* (Examine pagan Hindu worship mantra of TM,
oga, meditation, séances, Mary Worth, Hare Krishna, etc.) (b) *Have you
cently checked to see if such practices are occurring at your child's schools,
umber parties, and beach parties?* (c) *What did Jesus say about drawing
gh to God the Father, in John 14:6?*

(4) James 4:7-8. (a) *What promise do we have if we resist Satan?
an God's Word lie?* (b) *How can we resist Satan today?*

b. How to draw near to God.

(1) *Why do you feel it is important to take time to silently draw nigh
God before starting to pray, or don't you?*

(2) James 4:8. (a) *Have you ever felt God did not draw near to you
hen you tried to draw close to Him?* (b) *What hindrances could have been
the way?* (See Session 2.) *Could one of the occult practices mentioned
this session have been the cause?* (c) *Who was responsible for the sep-
ation, you or God?*

(3) Hebrews 11:6. (a) *How well do you know who the God in
aven is?* (b) *Do you feel you have an adequate mental picture of His
ity, power, love?* (c) *If not, what book will give you a complete view of
im?* Read Isaiah 6:1-3; Revelation 4:1-4; 8-11; James 1:17; Hebrews
:8; Psalm 116:5; Isaiah 40:28.

(4) Exodus 34:4, 29-35. (a) *Have you known anybody whose very
ce showed that he or she, like Moses, spent much time drawing close to*

God in heaven? (b) *Do you feel anybody ever thinks that of you?*

5. Make sure you as leader have some prayer requests to mention durin prayertime after you have led groups in drawing nigh to God.

Pray as Members of Christ's Body, the Church

1. Keep groups together for prayer time with leader directing all the praying.

2. Practice drawing nigh to God. (a) Have individuals in each grou confess aloud any sins that will keep them from drawing close to God. B sure to include any involvement in occult practices. (Use discretion in iden tifying sins that are very personal.) (b) Leader, read aloud Isaiah 6:1- and Revelation 4:1-4, 8-11, explaining first that they are to draw nigh t God in the silence that will follow the reading. Encourage them to form mental picture of God in heaven from the Scriptures. (c) Allow a full minut of silence for drawing nigh to God. (d) Ask each member to pray a one sentence adoration (who He is) prayer based on this or other Scripture. (e Leader, give one prayer request at a time for intercessory prayer in th groups. (See six-S method, session 5.)

Pray in Secret

Each person should record Isaiah 6:1-8; Revelation 4:1-4, 8-11; 5:6-1

Chalkboard 7
Worship is:
1. Seeking God
2. Coming close to Him
3. Confessing sin
4. Bursting out in praise to Him

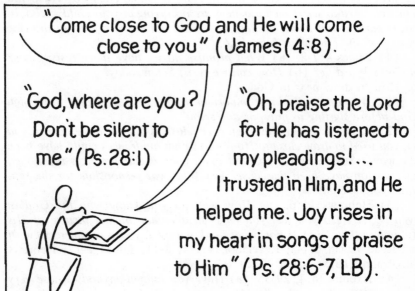

"Come close to God and He will come close to you" (James (4:8).

"God, where are you? Don't be silent to me" (Ps. 28:1)

"Oh, praise the Lord for He has listened to my pleadings!... I trusted in Him, and He helped me. Joy rises in my heart in songs of praise to Him" (Ps. 28:6-7, LB).

his notebook. Suggest waiting on God in silence every day this week. Give
each individual a copy of the following: (1) Worship the Lord, using the
words of Isaiah 6:3. (2) Consider how you would feel if you were actually
in God's presence (which you are). Pray verse 5. (3) Accept the Lord's
cleansing and be prepared to hear His voice of instruction through His Word
vv. 6-8). (4) Move on to Revelation 4—5. Keep your attention on God
and on the Lamb of God. Write down the words that describe God. Worship
Him. Pour out your heart to Him. (5) God is _____.
Fill in how you would describe Him.)

Assignment
Read chapter 10 of the text. Bring your MTM notebook to class.

SESSION **11**

The Horizontal Dimension of Prayer / *Text, Chapter 10*

Determine Your Goals
To find the visible results of prayer here on Planet Earth, to study methods
of intercessory prayer, and to discover that faith is the prerequisite to answered prayer.

Preparation
Read chapter 10 again, making careful notes of the points you want to
bring out later with the group. List the prerequisites of effective prayer on
flip chart, adding the new one for today—*faith*. Prepare or bring samples
of prayer letters, a prayer calendar, prayer lists, and other methods of intercessory prayer you may have. Bring blank calendar pages (one for each
group member) to be filled in with names during the session. Prepare chalkboard 8 and study MTM-11.

Examine and Share
1. Open the session with prayer. Ask the group if they can recall five prerequisites of effective prayer studied so far. As each one is mentioned, show
that prerequisite on the flip chart. They are: (a) Admitting and confessing
all sin; (b) Forgiving other people so God will forgive you; (c) Praying in
Jesus' name—prayer power for Christians only; (d) Praying in God's will;
(e) Drawing close to God.
Add today's prerequisite—*faith*. Quote Hebrews 11:6, emphasizing that
the pray-er must not only believe who God is (last session), but must also
believe that He is a Rewarder of them that diligently seek Him.

2. Display MTM-11.

    a. Have class members make their own triangle by holding up prayin hands (pressed together just above head level).

      (1) God is top of their praying hands (apex of MTM triangle).

      (2) Pray-er is at left elbow (lower right of MTM triangle).

      (3) Recipient of prayer at right elbow (lower right of MTM tr angle).

    b. The pray-er prays *up* (left arm) to God—who sifts requests accor(ing to His own will. Then God answers *down* (right arm) to recipient (prayer—in His own time.

    c. There never can be a horizontal dimension (results in the recipient unless request first goes *up* to God. Otherwise we are just trying to supe impose our will on somebody or something else.

3. Talk about the following methods of intercessory prayer while dis playing your samples (see *Text*).

    a. Individual intercessory prayer—in closet and all day and all nigh whenever you see a need.

    b. Prayer partner. What type of person makes a good prayer partner Do you qualify? (Always same sex unless mate, fiancé, or brother.)

    c. Prayer groups. (See six-S method, Session 5, *Text,* chapter 4.)

    d. Family. Devotions, with each child leaving in the morning.

    e. Church lists. (See chalkboard 8.)

    f. Prayertime. Setting specific time to pray, although not gathered i groups.

    g. Twenty-four hour prayer chains in churches. Each 15-minute o half-hour period of the whole 24-hour day (set alarms for night praying taken by one person or one couple each month, week or day, depending o how many people are involved. Makes continuous, unbroken prayer. Espe cially effective citywide with many churches.

    h. Telephone prayer chains—to be discussed next session.

    i. Prayer calendars. Hand out one sheet to each group membe Explain use.

4. Conduct a Bible study as follows:

    a. Discuss the following results that we humans see as the horizont dimension of prayer.

      (1) Unity—Acts 1:14. *Should Christians expect more unity whe they pray together than when they just work, meet in committees, or stud together? Why?*

      (2) Prayer transcends the miles—Philippians 1:4. Paul, in Rome prays for Christians in Philippi. Discuss other scriptural examples. *Have yo experienced our omnipresent God linking you in prayer with someone fa away? Has God answered your prayers for someone miles away?* Share.

      (3) Strangers—Matthew 6:8. *Do you think it is necessary to per sonally know the person for whom you are praying—far away or nearby Do you feel it imperative for you, in addition to God, to know all abou his needs for your prayers to be effective?*

      (4) Great in its workings—Hebrews 11:6. Discuss the prerequisit of faith as to God answering our prayers (James 1:6-7). *How is your fait*

in God's answering built up by keeping track of your specific prayer requests with dates and your specific answers with dates? Review answers to specific requests you have kept since Session 5 (MTM-5 prayer notebooks). Fill in answers other class members may know which you don't have recorded. (Review James 5:16b.) *Is the type of your requests changing—from just physical needs to include spiritual needs? If you want to see yourself and your church reaching out to win more people to Christ, what is the first step?*

(5) Prayer for all categories of needs: (a) Laborers—Matthew 9:36-38. (b) Those who need healing—James 5:16. (c) Those in authority —1 Timothy 2:1-2. (d) Those who despitefully use us—Matthew 5:44. (e) All other Christians—Ephesians 6:18-19. Suggest other scriptural examples.

b. Fill in blank calendars with name of one member on each day of coming week. Each person should be prayed for by a different person each day. (This is easily accomplished by each person starting with a different person and going around your circle in order.)

Pray as Members of Christ's Body, the Church
Pray in small groups with the leader announcing prayer topics. Observe the six S rules.
1. Draw nigh to God in a moment of silence (confessing sins if necessary).
2. Praise God for specific answers in your notebook from Session 5.
3. Pray new intercessory prayer requests (gathered by group leaders).
4. Promise God to faithfully pray for names on your new calendar each day this week.
5. Listen in silence as leader prays aloud for God to tell each class member which method or methods of intercessory prayer He wants them to start immediately.
6. Each member promises God to start doing what He said—immediately.

Pray in Secret
Pray each day for the person on your prayer calendar for that day.
Start any new method of intercession God laid on your heart during prayer.

Assignment
Read chapter 12. *Note change:* You studied chapter 11 for session 3.

Chalkboard 8
Use to demonstrate a prayer calendar.

Sun	Mon	Tues	Wed	Thurs	Fri	Sat
						Ann₁
Barb 2	Carol 3	Doris 4	Ellen 5	6	7	8
9	church board mtg. 10	11	12	13	14	15
16	17	18	19	20	21	22
23	24	25	26	27	28	29
30	31					

33

Telephone Prayer Chains / *Text, Chapter 12*

Determine Your Goals

To help people appreciate the effectiveness of telephone prayer chains and to teach how to organize them for churches, organizations, communities, or metropolitan areas.

Preparation

Reread chapter 12 carefully. Prepare a copy of MTM-12 for each group member (see "Other Uses of Transparency Masters," *Ditto Masters,* center of *Guide*). Have prayer chain sign-up cards for each group member including name, address, telephone number, and church affiliation.

Examine and Share

1. Have group share specific blessings from this prayer study in their own lives, families, churches, and other organizations. Begin with prayer.

2. Ask the group to report any new or enlarged methods of intercessory prayer God has laid on their hearts since the last session, what they have done to implement them during the past week, and what their future plans and desires are. Interact with helpful suggestions.

3. Introduce the last method of intercessory prayer: *telephone prayer chains.* General information includes:

a. The secret of the power of the chain is that all members, though not gathered together, can pray *simultaneously* for a need.

b. The chairperson makes or breaks the chain. Must be a respected Christian who can discern what details it is wise to send through the chain, can help word requests briefly and clearly, and is available for receiving calls during the specified hours.

c. Set the specific cut-off hour for receiving requests (except emergencies), so the chairperson can send them through and members will not wait needlessly for a call.

d. Members sign up for either the day or evening chain.

e. Approximately 10 persons per prayer chain. If more than 10 people, divide into chains of not more than 10 according to geographic location, time of day they want to receive calls, or by different churches, organizations, and so forth.

f. If it will be a large metropolitan prayer chain (up to 1,000), have regional directors under the chairperson, captains under directors, and several individual chains of 10 under the captains.

g. Make all prayer requests short.

h. Never send more than four requests per day (except emergency). If extremely important, send a request through alone.

i. Have organizational meeting where *each member* (1) signs rules and (2) prays a short prayer of commitment to God, promising Him to call and pray immediately when a request is received.

j. Meet regularly with all members of the prayer chains to pray together, thus keeping interest alive and the purpose of the chain clear. Questions can be answered and problems worked out at these meetings.

4. Teach point by point through the *Rules for Prayer Chain Members*—MTM-12.

5. Role play with a chairperson, person calling in a request, chairperson helping to word request (make sure it is a request not an answer), members of group chain receiving request, writing it down, dialing immediately (occasionally nobody home), and then praying immediately. Then call through the answer for prayer of thanks and praise to God.

6. Divide into groups for Bible study and discuss:

a. Philippians 4:6. *What kinds of prayer requests should go over a prayer chain?* Discuss physical and spiritual needs, using discretion, and thanking for answers.

b. Galatians 6:2. *Could this admonition be fulfilled by the use of a telephone prayer chain? How? What types of burdens can best be borne on telephone prayer chains?* (Discuss concrete examples.)

c. Matthew 9:36-38. *How could prayer chains be used to get laborers for Christ's work? Who could use it?* (Pastor, Christian Education director, club workers, Sunday School superintendents, Bible study teachers, hostesses or baby-sitter recruiters) *How do you feel you could convince these people to call on the prayer chain when a need for laborers arises?*

d. 1 Timothy 2:1-2. *What current needs does the president of the United States (or your country's leader) have, about which your prayer chain could pray? Your local officials, school board, etc?* Be specific.

e. Ephesians 6:18-19. *What kinds of problems and needs for all the saints (Christians) should be prayed for on telephone chains?*

Pray as Members of Christ's Body, the Church

Divide into prayer groups, with a leader directing prayer.

Draw nigh to God, confessing sins if necessary.

Listen in silence after leader prays, asking God to speak to each member about being on a telephone prayer chain.

Pray aloud in groups, one at a time, promising God to do whatever He has laid on your heart.

Spend time in intercessory prayer using the six-S method with requests volunteered from members.

Leader, close in prayer, thanking God for the privilege the class has had of studying and experiencing new heights in prayer.

Sign Up Those Who Want to Start a Telephone Prayer Chain

1. If an available chain already exists in community, church, or organi-

zation, you may want to encourage signing up on that one.

2. If not, organize a telephone prayer chain among the members of the group.

    a. Collect signed cards.

    b. Divide into chains.

    c. Decide on time of day for requests to be sent through.

    d. Set date for organizational meeting where you will:

        (1) Provide members with request and answer notebook (see Session 5). Have each member promise God aloud in prayer to pray and call faithfully.

        (2) Have each member sign rule sheet, promising God to abide by rules.

SESSION 13

Review

Alternative No. 1

Discussion Go back through the leader's guide and select discussion questions that will give an overview of the material.

Alternative No. 2

Question-answer You may choose to open the meeting for questions by having any member ask about something mentioned in the study that he didn't understand. As often as possible, solicit ideas from the group rather than answer all the questions yourself. Their responses may serve as feedback of what you taught, and give you an opportunity to correct wrong impressions.

Looking Ahead

As an encouragement to other members of the group, call for volunteers to tell what specific goals they have set for themselves as a result of this course. They may either state them as resolutions or as prayer requests. Close in prayer.